Fun Things to Do with Egg Cartons

by Kara L. Laughlin

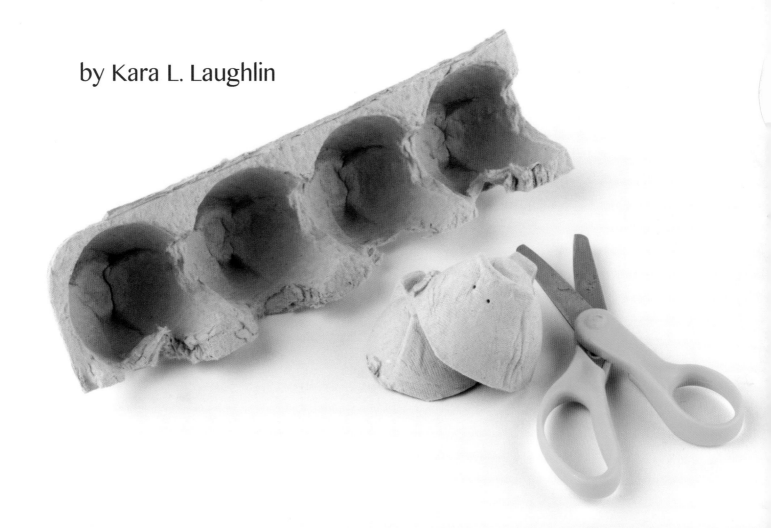

A+ Books are published by Capstone Press,
1710 Roe Crest Drive, North Mankato, Minnesota 56003
www.capstonepub.com

Library of Congress Cataloging-in-Publication Data
Laughlin, Kara L.
Fun Things to Do with Egg Cartons / by Kara L. Laughlin.
pages cm.—(Fun Things to Do. A+ Books)
Audience: Age 5–8.
Audience: K to grade 3.
Includes bibliographical references.
Summary: "Full-color photos and simple, step-by-step instructions describe 10 crafts and activities that reuse
egg cartons and common materials found around the house"—Provided by publisher.
ISBN 978-1-4765-9896-3 (hardcover)
ISBN 978-1-4765-9900-7 (ebook pdf)
1. Egg carton craft—Juvenile literature. I. Title.
TT870.5.L38 2015
745.5—dc23   2014012750

Editorial Credits
Jeni Wittrock, editor; Bobbie Nuytten, designer; Sarah Schuette, photo stylist; Marcy Morin, studio scheduler;
Kim Braun, project production; Tori Abraham, production specialist

Photo Credits
Images by Capstone Studio: Karon Dubke except Shutterstock: Calvste, 10, gregg williams, 16, Marques, 8 (top),
metrue 24 (bottom)

Printed in the United States of America in
North Mankato, Minnesota
112014   008604R

Table of Contents

Introduction

When you've eaten all the eggs in your fridge, what do you do with the carton? Throw it away? No way!

The crafts and activities in this book reuse egg cartons for art and play. Many of the projects work best with paper pulp egg cartons. If you need to get your hands on more pulp cartons, ask your friends.

You'll see "egg cups" or "spikes" in some of the directions. The cup is the place where the egg sits. The spike is the taller support between cups.

If cutting is too tricky, use a paintbrush to dab water where you want the cut. The water makes the egg carton soft. Then you can tear off what you need. But be sure to let everything dry before you move on to the craft.

Have fun reusing egg cartons with these *egg*citing projects. When you're done, make up some new projects of your own!

Inchworm Puppet

Supplies

» strip of 6 egg carton cups
» paints
» paintbrush
» scrapbook paper
» white glue
» chenille stems
» stick-on wiggle eyes
» 2 straws
» stapler

1. Fold each egg cup back and forth a few times. This makes your worm easy to bend.

2. Paint your worm green.

3. Decorate your worm with scrapbook paper or paint. Stick on the eyes.

4. Poke two holes in the first cup. Use chenille stems to make the inchworm's antennas.

5. Staple straws inside the front and back cups.

6. To make your worm crawl, move the straws together, then apart.

Step it Up: Make an inchworm life cycle play. Add fabric or paper plates to another inchworm to make it into a moth. Use a whole egg carton for a cocoon.

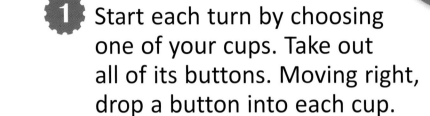

Mancala

Supplies

» 1 egg carton bottom
» 36 buttons or other small items
» 2 bowls
» a friend

Goal

Get as many buttons as you can into your bowl.

Setup

» Place a bowl at each end of the egg carton. Put three buttons in each cup.
» Sit across from your friend with the board (egg carton) sitting lengthwise between you. The cups on your side are yours. So is the bowl to your right.

Winning

The player with the most buttons in her bowl wins.

How To Play

1 Start each turn by choosing one of your cups. Take out all of its buttons. Moving right, drop a button into each cup.

If you reach your bowl, add a button. Go around the board, adding buttons to your friend's cups too.

If the last button lands in your bowl, take another turn. If not, it is your friend's turn.

2 Later in the game, you may reach your friend's bowl. Never drop buttons in your friend's bowl. Just skip it.

3 If the last button lands in an empty cup, take that button and all the buttons in the cup across from it. Put them in your bowl.

4 Take turns with your friend until there are no buttons on one side of the board. Who has the most buttons?

Step it Up: When you've mastered three buttons, try four or five buttons per cup.

Owl Mask

Supplies

» scissors
» egg carton
» paints
» paintbrush
» craft feathers
» craft glue
» pencil
» tape

1 Cut out a piece of egg carton with two egg cups and a spike.

2 Use the pencil to poke a hole in the bottom of each cup to make eyes.

3 Paint the eyes (the insides of the cups) and the beak (spike).

4 Glue some feathers around the eyes.

5 To hold your mask, tape a pencil to the side.

Step it Up: Make masks with friends, then play Owls and Mice. The mice hold flashlights (the sun) in a dark room. The owls try to sneak up on the mice. If a mouse shines a light on an owl, the owl must go to sleep (freeze). If an owl tags a mouse, they trade places.

Print a Tee

Supplies

» egg cartons
» T-shirt
» big piece of cardboard
» acrylic or fabric paint
» paintbrush

1 Place the cardboard inside the T-shirt. This keeps the surface flat and smooth.

2 Cut carton into pieces of 1, 2, 3, or 4 cups for different patterns. Paint the bottom of each cup.

3 Press the cups onto the shirt in any design you like. Gently peel them off.

4 Repeat as many times as you like.

5 Let paint dry completely.

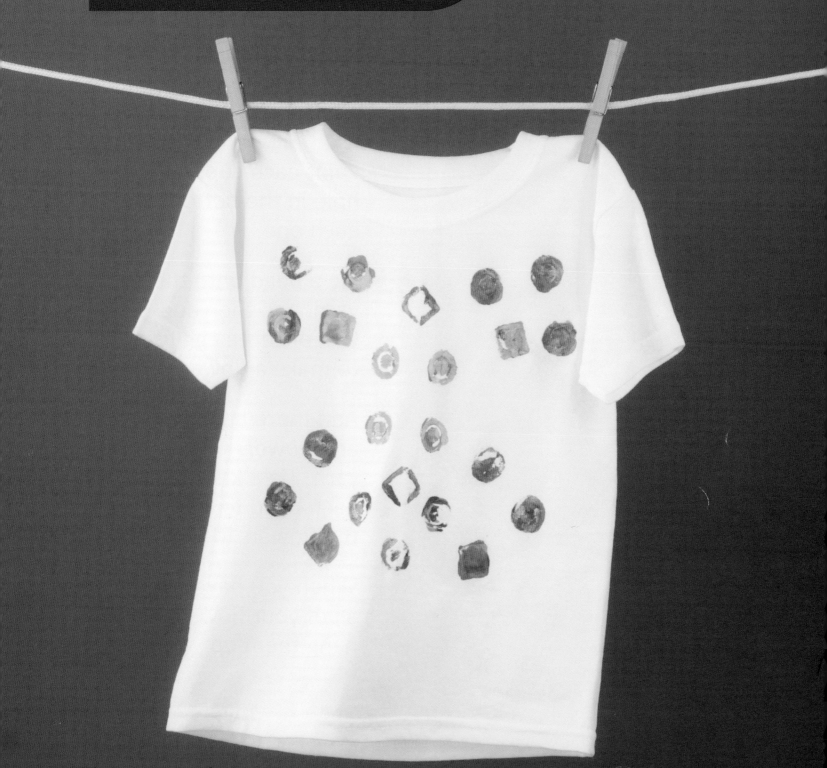

Step it Up: Cut the carton in pieces to make different prints. See if you can spell out your school's name!

Daisy Chains

Supplies

» egg cartons
» green yarn or string
» pencil
» plastic beads
» paint
» paintbrush

1. Cut apart the egg cups. Make four cuts in each cup for petals.

2. Paint each cup. Poke a hole in the bottom of each one.

3. Tie a bead onto the yarn, and then add two or three egg cups to make a flower.

4. Add more beads and flowers to the yarn. Tie a knot after each bead to keep the flowers in place.

5. When you have strung all of your flowers, hang them up.

Step it Up: Hang strings of flowers in your closet to turn it into a rain forest!

15

Robin Rest Stop

Supplies

» 1 egg carton bottom
» hole punch
» ribbon or strong string
» birdseed
» decorations

1. Punch a hole in the middle of each end of the egg carton.

2. Tie a string through each hole, then tie the strings together at the top.

3. Decorate the rest stop however you like.

4. Fill up the cups with birdseed.

5. Hang the rest stop from a tree branch or deck railing.

Be sure to bring your robin rest stop inside before storms!

Step it Up: Fill some of the cups with thread, strings, peanut butter, or suet. Watch to see what the birds like best. Do they like different things at different times of year?

Light-Up Lantern

Supplies

- » 3 lids from egg cartons with holes on the top
- » orange or yellow tissue paper or cellophane
- » scissors
- » glue or tape
- » string
- » paper plate
- » paintbrush
- » paint
- » plastic tea light
- » plastic tub

1. Glue or tape tissue paper or cellophane to the inside of the carton to cover the holes.

2. Glue the long sides together to make a column shaped like a triangle.

3. Poke string through a paper plate to make a handle.

4. Glue the paper plate to the top of the column.

5. Paint the lantern. Let dry.

6. Set a tea light on the plastic tub. Set the lantern over the tea light. Dim the lights and watch it glow.

Step it Up: Make a few lanterns and have a sunset picnic. Be sure the plastic tea lights are turned on inside the lantern. Then glue on the bottoms. Hang the lanterns by the picnic table.

Cheep Tricks

Supplies

» 2 egg-carton bottoms
» yellow and brown paint
» paintbrush
» craft paper or construction paper
» black marker
» craft feathers
» stick-on wiggle eyes
» shredded paper
» several coins or other small objects

1. Cut out six egg cups from the bottom of an egg carton.

2. Paint or decorate the six egg cups with yellow craft paper. These are your chicks.

3. Glue a construction paper beak and two wings to each chick.

4. Glue a craft feather on top of each cup.

5. Attach two wiggle eyes above each chick's beak.

5 Paint the second egg carton brown. Let it dry.

6 Add shredded paper to each egg cup in the second carton.

Step it Up: Pick a friend to play a guessing game! In secret put beads, pennies, beans, or other small objects in one row of six nests in the carton. Give your friend five seconds to study the pattern, then cover the nests with the chicks. See if your friend can remember the order of the objects. After she guesses, move the chicks off the nests to see if she was right!

5

Spin a Spaceship

Supplies

» paper cup
» 4 egg-carton cups
» paint
» paintbrush
» craft glue
» pencil
» stickers in different shapes and colors
» colored paper
» cellophane (optional)

This spaceship is a wind catcher! The egg cups catch the wind and spin the spaceship.

1 Paint four egg cups.

2 Glue the four egg cups around the outside of the paper cup. They need to be near the rim with the egg cup bottoms facing right.

3 Poke a small hole through the bottom of the paper cup.

Step it Up: Try other designs. You can use paper bowls, plates, and small boxes for ships. Use as many egg cups as you need to make them spin.

5

4 Put the cup upside down on a pencil. The point of the pencil should go in the hole.

5 Cut out a window for your spaceship. Use paper and stickers to make lights, aliens, and stars.

6 Take your finished spaceship outside on a breezy day. Hold the pencil and watch it spin in the wind.

Hang a Star

Supplies

- » small container with a lid
- » bottom half of a paper egg carton
- » 1/2 cup (118 milliliters) water
- » 1/2 cup (64 grams) flour
- » 1 teaspoon (5 milliliters) craft glue
- » 1 teaspoon (5 milliliters) salt
- » star-shaped cookie cutter
- » towel
- » paints
- » paintbrush
- » ribbon or string

1 Rip egg carton into small pieces and set aside.

2 Add water and flour to container. Seal the lid and shake the mixture until there are no lumps.

3 Mix in egg carton pieces. Let the mixture sit for at least four hours.

4 When mushy, add craft glue and stir. Add salt and stir.

5 Squeeze the mixture with your hands to get most of the water out. Press into cookie cutter on a towel.

6 Remove cookie cutter right away. Let star dry at least 24 hours.

7 Paint your star. Let paint dry.

8 Use a dab of glue to add a loop of ribbon to the back for hanging.

7

Step it Up: Make sprouting stars! Leave out the salt and add marigold seeds to the mix before shaping. Don't paint your star. Instead, when it is dry, give it to a friend. Your friend can plant it in soil, water it, and watch it grow!

Read More

Laughlin, Kara. *Fun Things to Do with Paper Plates and Paper Cups.* Fun Things to Do. North Mankato, Minn.: Capstone, 2015.

Richmond, Margie Hayes. *Look What You Can Make with Egg Cartons.* Look What You Can Make. Honesdale, Penn.: Highlights Press, 2013.

Warwick, Ellen. *50 Ways to Get Your CartOn: Recycle and Create Milk and Egg Carton Crafts that Rock.* New York: Sterling Innovation, 2010.

Internet Sites

FactHound offers a safe, fun way to find Internet sites related to this book. All of the sites on FactHound have been researched by our staff.

Here's all you do:

Visit *www.facthound.com*

Type in this code: 9781476598963

Super-cool stuff! Check out projects, games and lots more at www.capstonekids.com